6×7/11 LT 12/09

6×7/11 LT 12/09

In the Footsteps of Explorers

James Cook

The Pacific Coast and Beyond

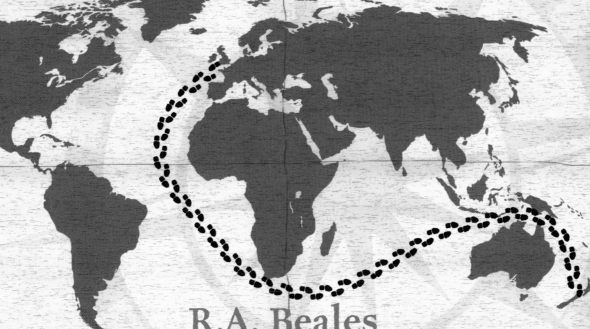

R.A. Beales

Crabtree Publishing Company
www.crabtreebooks.com

Crabtree Publishing Company

www.crabtreebooks.com

Thanks to my brother, Bernard Beales,
for his help in the preparation of this book.

Coordinating editor: Ellen Rodger
Series editor: Carrie Gleason
Project editor: Rachel Eagen
Editor: Adrianna Morganelli
Design and production coordinator: Rosie Gowsell
Cover design, layout, and production assistance: Samara Parent
Art direction: Rob MacGregor
Scanning technician: Arlene Arch-Wilson
Photo research: Allison Napier

Consultants: Stacy Hasselbacher and Tracey L. Neikirk, Museum Educators, The Mariners' Museum

Photo Credits: akg- Images: cover; The Art Archive: pp. 10-11, pp. 16-17, pp. 22-23; The Art Archive/ Musée des Arts Décoratifs Paris/ Dagli Orti: p. 25; Bibliotheque Nationale, Paris, France, Lauros/ Giraudon / Bridgeman Art Library: pp. 28-29; Philip Mould, Historical Portraits Ltd., London, UK/ Bridgeman Art Library: p. 8 (top); Private Collection/ Bridgeman Art Library: p. 21; Bettmann/ Corbis: p. 7, p. 24 (top); Free Agents Limited/ Corbis: pp. 14-15; Frans Lanting/ Corbis: p. 30; Neil Rabinowitz/ Corbis: p. 24 (bottom); Underwood & Underwood/ Corbis: p. 26; John Van Hasselt/ Corbis Sygma: p. 31; The Granger Collection, New York: p. 9, p. 29; Mark Antman/ The Image Works: p. 8 (bottom); The British Museum/ HIP/ The Image Works: p. 27; Jeff Greenberg/ The Image Works: p. 23. Other images from stock photo cd

Illustrations: Lauren Fast: p. 6; Dennis Gregory Teakle: p. 4; David Wysotski: pp. 18-19.

Cartography: Jim Chernishenko: title page, p. 12

Cover: Captain Cook brought artists on his voyages to make drawings of the new species of plants and animals they found.

Title page: Captain Cook explored many Pacific islands during three long sea voyages. His discoveries led to the building of permanent European settlements.

Sidebar icon: Cook and his crew discovered many exotic species of plants and animals during their travels. In Hawaii, they found many different colorful butterflies and birds.

Crabtree Publishing Company

www.crabtreebooks.com   1-800-387-7650

Cataloging-in-Publication Data
Beales, R. A. (Richard A.), 1956-
    James Cook : the Pacific coast and beyond / written by R.A. Beales.
        p. cm. -- (In the footsteps of explorers)
    Includes index.
    ISBN-13: 978-0-7787-2415-5 (rlb)
    ISBN-10: 0-7787-2415-8 (rlb)
    ISBN-13: 978-0-7787-2451-3 (pbk)
    ISBN-10: 0-7787-2451-4 (pbk)
    1. Cook, James, 1728-1779--Juvenile literature. 2. Explorers--Great Britain--Biography--Juvenile literature. 3. Islands of the Pacific--Discovery and exploration--Juvenile literature.   I. Title. II. Series.
    G246.C7B385 2005
    910'.92--dc22   2005014942
                                                                    LC

Published in
the United States
PMB 16A
350 Fifth Ave.
Suite 3308
New York, NY
10118

Published
in Canada
616 Welland Ave.
St. Catharines
Ontario, Canada
L2M 5V6

Published in the
United Kingdom
73 Lime Walk
Headington
Oxford
OX3 7AD
United Kingdom

Published
in Australia
386 Mt. Alexander Rd.
Ascot Vale (Melbourne)
VIC 3032

Contents

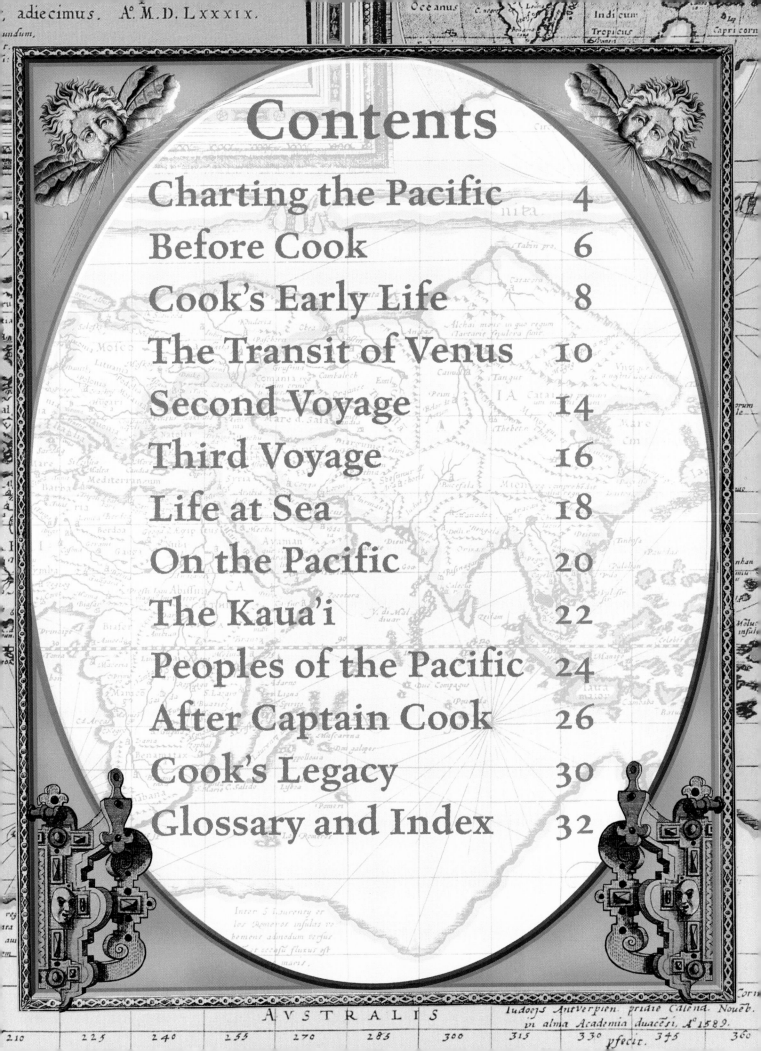

Charting the Pacific

Captain James Cook was a British navy officer who lived in the 1700s. His journeys in the Pacific Ocean brought him to New Zealand, Hawaii, Alaska, and the East Coast of Australia.

In Love with the Sea

Cook took to a life at sea as a young man. As a teenager, he **apprenticed** to a sea captain and learned the basics of **navigation**. Cook eventually joined the British Royal Navy, and showed natural skill as a sailor. By the time he was 30 years old, he made his first overseas trip to Canada. The Royal Navy was so impressed with Cook's seamanship that they hired him to look for land they believed lay south in the Pacific Ocean.

Three Voyages

Cook and his crews made three Pacific voyages. They drew maps of the places they explored, and sketches of the plants and animals that were native to these places. Cook and his crews also encountered peoples that were unknown to other Europeans at the time. They recorded their observations in **log books.**

Opening up the Pacific

Before Cook's voyages, many Europeans believed that the Pacific was a paradise where mysterious creatures lived. Cook's reports helped Europeans to understand what the Pacific islands were really like. Many Europeans built **colonies** there after Cook's voyages.

Captain James Cook became a skilled sailor when he was only a teenager.

Kangaroo

In the Pacific, Cook and his crew found many different plant and animal **species** that they had never seen back home in England. Scientists accompanied Cook on his voyages to observe, take samples, and make sketches of these new species. In Australia, Cook and his crew saw a kangaroo for the first time. They described the animal in the following journal:

"The head neck and shoulders of this Animal was very small in proportion to the other parts; the tail was nearly as long as the body, thick next the rump and tapering towards the end...progression by hopping or jumping 7 or 8 feet at each hop upon its hind legs only, for in this it makes no use of its fore, which seem to be only design'd for scratching in the ground... The skin is cover'd with a short hairy fur of a dark Mouse or Grey Colour. Excepting the head and ears which I thought was something like a Hare's, it bears no sort of resemblance to any European Animal I ever saw; it is said to bear much resemblance to the Gerbua (gerbil) excepting in size..."

-October 27, 1728-

James Cook is born in Yorkshire, England.

-1768 to 1771-

First Pacific voyage

-1772 to 1775-

Second voyage

-1776 to 1780-

Third voyage

-February 14, 1779-

Cook dies in Hawaii.

-1271-
Venetian explorer Marco Polo (above) travels to China, bringing back tales of great wealth.

-1488-
Portuguese explorer Bartolomeu Dias rounds the southernmost tip of Africa, called the Cape of Good Hope.

-1498-
Portuguese explorer Vasco da Gama becomes the first European to sail from Europe to India.

Before Cook

In the late 1400s, Europeans began exploring unknown seas and lands, thirsty for knowledge about their world. They hoped to claim new territories for their kings and queens, make scientific discoveries, and become wealthy.

Age of Exploration

The voyages of explorers Marco Polo and Christopher Columbus had made Europeans aware that great riches could be found outside of Europe. Merchants began traveling to China, India, and the Moluccas, or Spice Islands, to seek valuable **trade goods**. Gold, silk, and spices were all desired by wealthy Europeans. After Christopher Columbus made his first voyage to the **New World**, European kings and queens hired other explorers to claim land and build colonies there.

Colonies and Wealth

Around 1500, Spanish, Dutch, French, and English colonies were set up in the West Indies, or Caribbean, as well as in parts of North, South, and Central America. The colonists farmed food crops on the rich soil and forced the native peoples to work in gold mines. Gold jewelry made by the native peoples, livestock, and other products were sent back to Europe and sold in markets. European colonists became very wealthy this way.

Pepper, cloves, and cinnamon were popular spices in Europe during the Age of Exploration.

6

During the 1600s and 1700s, European traders often encountered pirate ships along important trade routes. Pirates robbed ships of their trade goods, such as gold, silver, and gems. Several pirates are famous today, but they were feared as dangerous criminals when they were alive.

The Unknown Southern Continent

A Greek **astronomer** named Claudius Ptolemy made many speculations about the world around 300 A.D. Centuries later, European mapmakers used Ptolemy's ideas to draw maps of the world. Ptolemy believed that a large continent covered the southern quarter of the world and anchored the rest of the land of the globe. Ptolemy called this continent *Terra Australis Incognita*, which means "Unknown Southern Continent." Europeans viewing the maps during the Age of Exploration believed the land was a warm, civilized paradise rich with gold, jewels, fruits, and other delicious foods.

Cook's Early Life

As a teenager, Cook worked as an apprentice to Captain John Walker in the port of Whitby, England. Cook lived with the Walker family and worked on coal ships called colliers. He was taught how to rig a boat, and how to navigate using mathematical calculations.

In the Navy

Walker eventually offered Cook a ship of his own to command, but Cook decided to join the British Royal Navy instead. He became an ordinary seaman, the lowest rank. Cook was an outstanding sailor and was promoted to higher ranks within the navy. He became a navigational officer onboard the *HMS Pembroke*, in which he helped chart the St. Lawrence River, in present-day Canada. He then joined two more voyages to map the coast of Newfoundland.

(left) Captain John Walker taught James Cook the basics of navigation while Cook served as an apprentice on Walker's coal ships.

(below) Cook's maps of the St. Lawrence River were so accurate that sailors used them for over 100 years.

Captain James Cook observed the Venus eclipse from an astronomy tent.

The Transit of Venus

Astronomer Edmund Halley predicted that on June 3, 1769, the planet Venus would cross the sun's path. Scientists from many countries were sent to different parts of the world to view the **eclipse**. The Royal Navy made Cook a **lieutenant**, and sent him to the Pacific island of Tahiti to observe the eclipse. Cook was chosen because of a detailed report he had written about a previous eclipse while in Newfoundland.

Making Preparations

Cook traveled aboard a collier, or "cat," which the Royal Navy purchased and renamed the *Endeavour*. The voyage was well recorded. Astronomer Charles Green and artist Sydney Parkinson joined the expedition in order to observe and record the eclipse in journals and sketches. Scientist Joseph Banks also joined the voyage. Banks was especially interested in botany, the study of plants. He sketched the plants and wildlife they saw on the voyage.

-July 15, 1755-

Cook turns down a promotion with John Walker and joins the Royal Navy.

-1757 to 1760-

Cook becomes a navigational officer onboard the *HMS Pembroke*.

-1762-

Cook maps the coast of Newfoundland, in present-day Canada.

The Transit of Venus

The *Endeavour* set sail from Plymouth, England. In addition to viewing the eclipse, the British Royal Navy assigned Cook a second, secret mission. After viewing the eclipse, Cook was to head south to look for *Terra Australis Incognita,* or the Unknown Southern Continent.

At Sea

The *Endeavour* stopped in Spain for food and **provisions**, then crossed the Atlantic and landed in Rio de Janeiro, in the South American country of Brazil. There, Cook and his men were suspected of being pirates by the country's **viceroy**. Guards followed the crew wherever they went. Banks, the ship's scientist, **bribed** some of the Spanish soldiers and snuck inland to study the local plant life.

Into the Pacific

The expedition continued south and around the tip of South America, then continued southwest into the Pacific. The ship passed through the region where the famous geographer Alexander Dalrymple had speculated that the Unknown Southern Continent was located. Cook did not find this imaginary land.

At Tahiti

The *Endeavour* sailed on and eventually anchored at Matavai Bay, Tahiti. The crew found groves of fruits unknown to them, including coconuts and bananas, as well as colorful butterflies and lizards. The Tahitians tattooed their bodies, which the English had never seen before. Joseph Banks had his arm tattooed, starting the tradition of tattoos for sailors.

Viewing the Eclipse

Cook and his crew built an **observatory** at Tahiti and set up a camp on the beach for viewing the eclipse. This camp became known as Fort Venus. A hazy glow surrounding Venus made it difficult to see. After leaving Tahiti, they sailed southwest until they spotted the two islands that are now known as the north and south islands of New Zealand.

(background) Cook landing on a Pacific island. Not all of Cook's encounters with the Aboriginal peoples were peaceful.

-August 26, 1768-

Cook departs England.

-April 11, 1769 -

Cook arrives at Matavai Bay.

-June 3, 1769-

Cook observes the transit of Venus.

-April 29, 1770-

Cook and crew land at Botany Bay, Australia.

-July 12, 1771-

The *Endeavour* returns to England.

At New Zealand

The Aboriginal peoples of New Zealand, the Maori, were warriors who traveled in large canoes carved from trees. Historians believe that the ancestors of the Maori traveled great distances in these canoes, because they spoke a language that was similar to that of the Tahitians. Cook was amazed that the Maori traveled the Pacific Ocean without using modern navigational tools, such as compasses.

(below) Cook did not find the Unknown Southern Continent, but he mapped several Pacific islands and claimed new territory for Britain.

At Australia

The *Endeavour* sailed on and pulled into a harbor on the East Coast of Australia. Banks and Cook were so fascinated by all of the varieties of plants they found growing there that they named it Botany Bay. The people from this part of Australia had never seen Europeans before, and were not interested in trading with them. Cook and his men eventually made their way up the East Coast, and ran the ship right into the Great Barrier Reef, the world's largest **coral reef.**

(above) Banks found many exotic species in Australia, such as Bird of Paradise flowers.

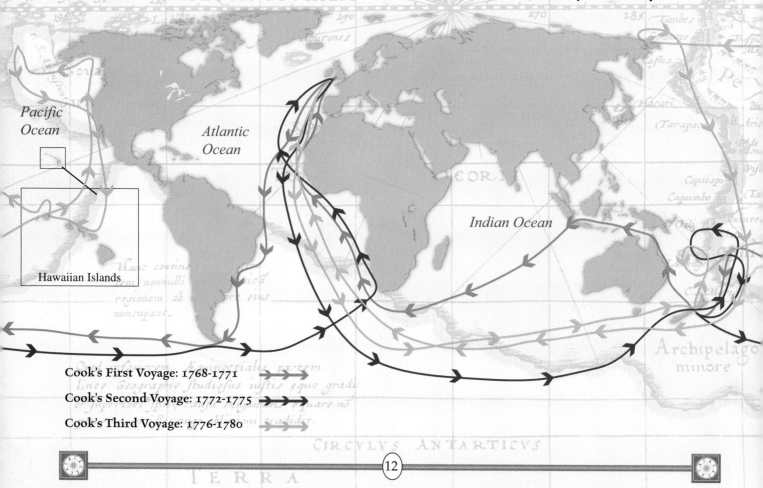

Pacific Ocean

Atlantic Ocean

Indian Ocean

Hawaiian Islands

Cook's First Voyage: 1768-1771
Cook's Second Voyage: 1772-1775
Cook's Third Voyage: 1776-1780

Stuck

The *Endeavour* was badly damaged on the reef and needed repairs. The crew fixed a large hole in the boat's hull, or body, with a patch that they made from rope, dung, and a piece of torn sail. They harvested and ate sea greens to prevent a common seafaring sickness called scurvy.

Laying Claim

Cook claimed the East Coast of Australia for England and named it New South Wales. The crew then headed northwest, following an **inlet** between Australia and New Guinea, and Cook named the route the Endeavour Strait, after the ship.

Homeward Bound

On their way back home, the crew stopped for supplies at a Dutch port town called Batavia in present-day Jakarta, Indonesia. Many of Cook's men became sick with **malaria** and **dysentery** at Batavia and died. Among the dead were the astronomer Charles Green and the artist Sydney Parkinson. By the time the crew returned to England, they had been at sea for almost three years.

While Cook and his crew repaired their ship, they saw giant sea turtles that weighed up to 300 pounds (136 kilograms), as well as flying fish called mudskippers.

Second Voyage

Cook's charts, maps, and journals from his voyage impressed the Admiralty, which controlled the Royal Navy. New lands had been claimed for Britain, including the East Coast of Australia and New Zealand. The Royal Navy ordered a second voyage to look for the Unknown Southern Continent.

Setting Sail

Cook set sail from Plymouth, England, this time with two ships under his command. Cook captained the *Resolution*, while Tobias Furneaux captained a smaller ship, the *Adventure*. They agreed to meet in New Zealand if the ships were separated. Two scientists and two astronomers came along to study new plants and animals, as well as the customs of the people they met.

Cook and his crew knew they were close to the Antarctic when they spotted penguins.

Freezing Waters

Cook sailed south and headed into the freezing waters of the Antarctic. The crew counted more than 100 icebergs in one day. The sails of the ships froze, and the ice-covered ropes cut the crew's hands as they hoisted the sails. Cook and his crew spotted whales, sea birds, and penguins as they approached Antarctica, a frozen continent close to where the Southern Continent was thought to be located. They were blocked by ice and had to steer north.

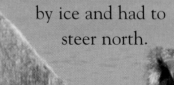

Pacific Adventures

Cook set sail for Tahiti to rest his crew, and then visited Tonga, a region discovered by the Dutch. Cook renamed Tonga the Friendly Islands. The ships then sailed further south to search for the Southern Continent, but they were separated in a storm. Cook waited for Furneaux to arrive in New Zealand, but eventually left because he thought the *Adventure* was not coming. Furneaux arrived a few days later, and ten of his crew members were killed in a fight with the Maori.

Going Home

Furneaux returned to England, but Cook continued his voyage and claimed several more islands, including Easter Island, New Hebrides, and New Caledonia. On the way back to England, Cook discovered an island group off the tip of South America. He named it South Georgia. It is now called Tierra del Fuego.

(background) Tahiti is a tropical island with many exotic species of birds, fruit, and flowers.

Third Voyage

Within a year of returning home, Cook was sent on a third Pacific voyage. He took two ships, the *Resolution* and the *Discovery*, to New Zealand, Hawaii, and up the coast of what is now British Columbia and Alaska. Cook never returned from this voyage.

Missions

King George III of England arranged for Cook to bring animals, such as cows, goats, and pigs, to the people of New Zealand and Tahiti. The king hoped that they would raise these animals, so that British settlers could use them when they returned to build colonies. The Admiralty ordered Cook to navigate a Northwest Passage, which was thought to link the Atlantic and Pacific oceans. This route would serve as a shortcut for traders to Asia.

Hawaii

After stopping in both New Zealand and Tahiti to present the people there with the **domesticated** animals, the *Resolution* headed north. Cook claimed Christmas Island north of Tahiti. Cook and his crew then became the first Europeans to land in Hawaii. The island chain was home to exotic birds, plants, and a generous people known as the Kaua'i. Cook soon left Hawaii to try to find the Northwest Passage. The crew followed the coast of Alaska to the Bering Strait, between Alaska and Russia, but were stopped by ice. Cook ordered the ships to return to Hawaii to rest the crew.

Return to Hawaii

Cook and his men were welcomed by the Kaua'i when they returned to Hawaii. They had arrived during the Kaua'i harvest festival, Makahiki. During the festival, the Kaua'i worshiped Lono, the Hawaiian god of the harvest. Cook and his crew attended feasts held in honor of Lono.

Suspicious of Cook

After the Makahiki celebrations, Cook left Hawaii to continue the voyage, but returned to the islands when the *Resolution*'s mast broke in a storm. This time, the Kaua'i were not happy to see the Europeans. Some historians believe the Kaua'i mistook Cook for their harvest god Lono when he arrived the first time. When he returned so suddenly, they realized he was not their god and thought he was trying to fool them. A fight between Cook and the Kaua'i ended in the death of Cook.

(background) Tension between the Kaua'i and Europeans ended in bloodshed.

-July 12, 1776-
Cook sets sail on his third voyage.

-January 18, 1778-
Cook discovers Hawaii.

-January 17, 1779-
Cook returns to Hawaii.

-February 14, 1779-
Cook is killed at Hawaii.

-October 4, 1780-
Resolution returns to England.

Life at Sea

Cook ran a tight ship, and kept order by punishing drunkenness, and requiring crew members to keep busy. Proper diet and cleanliness were also important in the prevention of disease.

Jobs Onboard

As captain, Cook held the highest position of authority. He was in charge of assigning duties to sailors, as well as charting the **course** for his ships. His orders were enforced by **marines**, who helped keep order. Topmen worked high up in the sails, making sure the sails were angled properly for sailing in the right direction at top speeds.

Sauerkraut

Sauerkraut was an excellent food to have onboard, because it is rich in vitamin C, and keeps without refrigeration for long periods of time. Here is a simple recipe to try. Ask an adult's help.

Ingredients:
6 pounds (3 kg) of cabbage
4 tablespoons (60 mL)of coarse salt
cold water

Directions:
1. Wash the cabbage and chop it very finely.
2. Place the cabbage in a bowl and add the salt, then mix together.
3. Pack the salted cabbage into clean mason jars. Top the jars with cold water and make sure there are no bubbles before screwing on the caps tightly.
4. Store for six to eight weeks before eating. Try the sauerkraut on top of hot dogs or ham.

Disease

Scurvy is a disease caused from a lack of vitamin C, which is found in fresh fruits and vegetables. Scurvy caused sailors' gums to swell, turn black, and eventually caused their teeth to fall out. In the worst cases, sailors died from scurvy. Scurvy was very common during the Age of Exploration, but Cook took strict measures to prevent scurvy onboard his ships. He forced his crew to eat sea greens, such as seaweed, whenever they found them growing on the shores of the places they explored. Not a single member of Cook's crew died from scurvy on any of his voyages, even though some of the voyages lasted for several years.

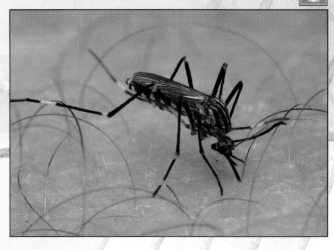

Disease-carrying mosquitoes were another risk for sailors. Bites from infected mosquitoes often brought diseases such as malaria, which is a life-threatening illness that causes high fevers.

(background) Sailors were expected to help with the overall running of the ship, including cleaning the ship, making repairs, and helping navigate. Cook is known for having kept a very clean ship. He made his crew air out their bedding, and he also checked their hands regularly to make sure they were clean.

On the Pacific

Cook sailed in large ships called colliers. Colliers were good for long voyages because they had a lot of space for storing items such as food and supplies. Colliers were sturdy ships that could sail in most weather, including rough seas and storms.

The Ships

The *Endeavour* had three masts, or sails, and three decks. It was 106 feet (32 meters) long and could hold about 85 sailors. The *Adventure* and the *Discovery* were also colliers, but they were smaller than the *Endeavour*. This allowed them to sail through narrow ocean inlets and come close to shore without running **aground**.

Cargo

The ship's hold is a storage space for food, weapons, clothes, and trade goods. Tools and metal objects, such as nails, were highly valued by the people of Tahiti, New Zealand, and Hawaii. Metal was not available on these islands, so the people there melted down the nails to make their own tools.

Meals

Food on long voyages spoiled quickly in the moist sea air, because ships did not have proper refrigeration. Salted meat, sauerkraut, and biscuits called hard tack were staple items on Cook's ships because they kept for a long time without rotting.

A sextant was used to measure the height of the stars above sea level.

Navigation

Cook and his crew used several devices to determine their location at sea. A ship's latitude, or distance north or south of the equator, could be calculated with a quadrant, which sailors used to compare the position of the stars to the position of the sea. Speed was measured by the time it took for an object in the water to float between two marked points on a ship. The ocean's current was measured by the angle at which the object floated in the water. On his second voyage, Cook took an early chronometer, an instrument for keeping track of time at sea.

(background) Cook liked to travel in colliers because they could sail in shallow waters close to shore, and carry a lot of supplies.

The Kaua'i

The Kaua'i of Hawaii had never encountered Europeans before Cook arrived with his crew. After a misunderstanding during Makahiki, the Kaua'i harvest festival, tensions mounted, resulting in the death of Captain James Cook.

Death of Cook

Some historians believe that the Kaua'i mistook Cook for one of their gods, Lono, who was honored during Makahiki. After leaving the island, Cook was forced to return after a mast broke on his ship. Some historians claim that the Kaua'i grew suspicious of Cook, as Lono was not supposed to return after Makahiki. The Kaua'i might have felt that Cook had betrayed them. After one of Cook's boats was stolen, Cook came ashore to confront the Kaua'i. A riot broke out, and Cook was stabbed to death. His crew fled back to the ships. After several days, the Kaua'i rowed out and returned some of the captain's bones. The rest of Cook's body had been **sacrificed** in a ceremony.

Daily Life

The Kaua'i were farmers and fishers. Their main crop was kalo, a potato-like plant. They also grew sweet potatoes and a starchy fruit called breadfruit. They ate fish and other marine life, such as green turtles. The Kaua'i built homes by weaving grass and palm leaves, and binding them together with mud.

(background) Cook's crew claimed that he was clubbed and stabbed after killing a Kaua'i man. The crew returned to England without their captain.

Peoples of the Pacific

Cook and his crew met many different peoples on the west coast of North America and the many Pacific islands they explored. They traded with a people they called the Nootka on Vancouver Island, and were treated to feasts on the South Pacific islands of Polynesia.

Tahitians

The Tahitians farmed crops and fished for food from the sea. They also hunted animals, such as wild pigs. The Tahitians traveled in double-hulled outrigger canoes. These boats were made of two tree logs that were hollowed out, then attached to each other with woven grass or palm leaves.

(above) The full-face tattoos show this man's high status. The Maori often removed the heads of their dead leaders, preserved them, and kept them as valued possessions.

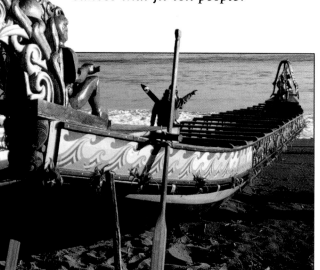

(below) The Maori and Tahitians traveled throughout the Pacific islands to trade and fish. Cook described the Nootka, or Aboriginal peoples of Vancouver, as having giant decorated canoes that fit ten people.

Maori

The Maori of New Zealand were proud warriors and great artists. They carved tools and ornaments from wood, bone, and stone. The Maori tattooed their faces and bodies with intricate swirling patterns. Some men, especially important chiefs, had their entire faces tattooed, while women were usually tattooed on their chin and lips. The Maori were excellent hunters.

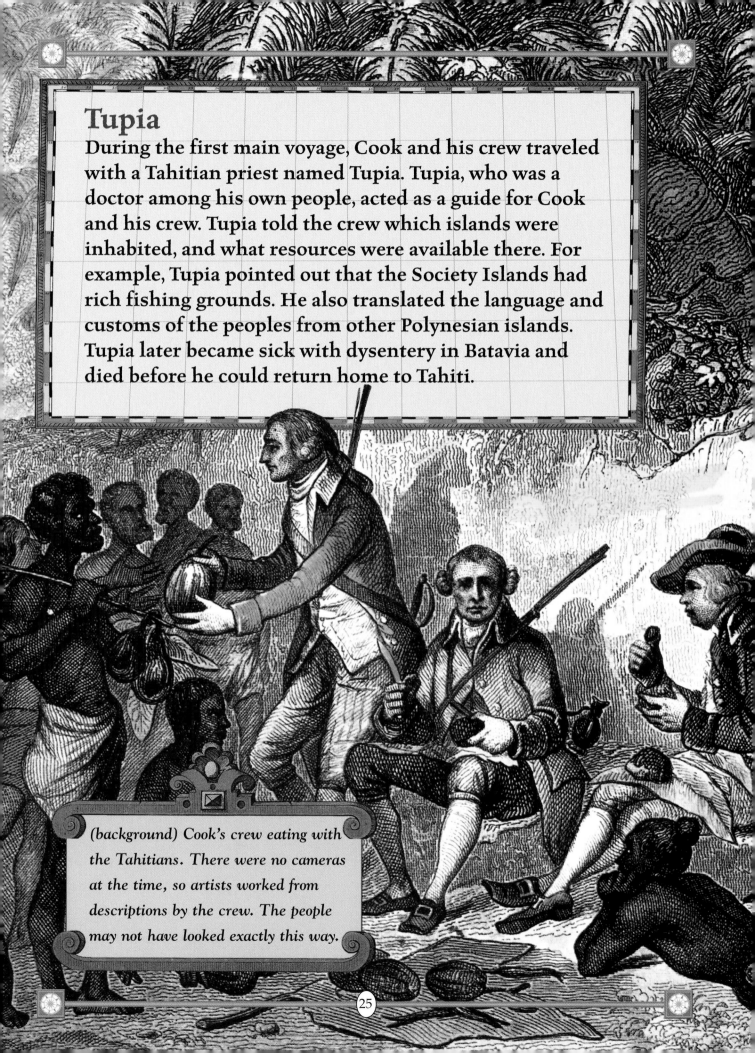

Tupia

During the first main voyage, Cook and his crew traveled with a Tahitian priest named Tupia. Tupia, who was a doctor among his own people, acted as a guide for Cook and his crew. Tupia told the crew which islands were inhabited, and what resources were available there. For example, Tupia pointed out that the Society Islands had rich fishing grounds. He also translated the language and customs of the peoples from other Polynesian islands. Tupia later became sick with dysentery in Batavia and died before he could return home to Tahiti.

(background) Cook's crew eating with the Tahitians. There were no cameras at the time, so artists worked from descriptions by the crew. The people may not have looked exactly this way.

After Captain Cook

Captain James Cook changed the way Europeans saw the world. He proved that there was no great southern paradise, but he also claimed that a landmass did exist at the South Pole.

The Unknown Southern Land

The landmass that Cook almost discovered turned out to be the frozen continent of Antarctica. While Antarctica is not a paradise of gold, gems, and delicious fruits, it is home to many interesting varieties of birds, seals, and whales. Many countries have scientific research stations there, including Australia, Chile, Argentina, the United States, and France.

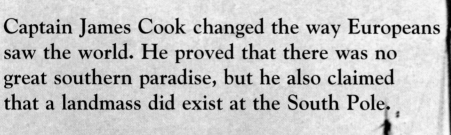

(background) Norwegian explorer Roald Amundsen was the first to reach the South Pole over a hundred years after Cook's final voyage.

What's in it For Us?

Antarctica was of no interest to European merchants. There were no people there to trade with, and no resources that could be sold back in Europe. Antarctica was also too cold to build colonies for people to live.

Opening up the Pacific

Roald Amundsen eventually navigated the Northwest Passage just north of Canada's mainland. Even though Cook did not find this route, his maps of the Pacific provided a better understanding of what the Pacific Ocean and its islands looked like. People now live on many of the Pacific islands that were uninhabited when Cook discovered them.

Changes to Pacific Life

Cook's visits to the Pacific islands were both good and bad for the people who lived there. He brought them domesticated animals such as sheep, pigs, goats, and cows. The animals provided meat for food and skins for clothing. The flood of European explorers that came to the Pacific after Cook brought diseases, such as smallpox, one of the world's most feared viruses, and tuberculosis, a lung disease. Countless people native to the South Pacific died as a result.

After Cook's explorations, the British began sending their criminals to Australia. This picture shows a group of convicts clearing the land to build a prison.

British Settlements

Cook's discovery of several Pacific islands caught the interest of other Europeans. Throughout the 1800s, many of the islands were colonized. The people who lived there first, came under the rule of the European settlers. Millions of people now live in the places that Cook discovered. Australia, New Zealand, and Hawaii all have large numbers of people from European **descent**.

(background) The colonization of Hawaii resulted in the loss of the traditional way of life of the Kaua'i.

Scientific Contribution

Cook's voyages were important to science. Cook's own contributions to mapmaking and navigation helped to shape future long-distance voyages. Joseph Banks was the first scientist to join an overseas expedition. His discoveries of plants and animals that were foreign to Europeans prompted other scientists to go to sea. Scientists became a standard part of ships' crews for long sea voyages.

Voyage to the Pacific Ocean

Cook wrote a book about his third voyage with James King, who captained the *Discovery* back to England after Cook's death. The book, *Voyage to the Pacific Ocean*, was based on their journals. British Christian minister William Carey was inspired by the book, and traveled to the Pacific to convert the people to Christianity. Other missionaries followed, settling in Australia, New Zealand, Hawaii, and Tahiti. They outlawed traditional celebrations and the belief in other gods.

Missionaries to the South Pacific tried to scrub off Maori facial tattoos with sandstone.

Several members of Cook's crew went on to play major roles in history.

-Joseph Banks-

Became president of the Royal Society.

-William Hodges-

Became the first European artist to visit India.

-George Vancouver-

Captained voyages to chart the northwest American coast.

29

Cook's Legacy

Cook's journals and maps of the Pacific islands and the surrounding sea helped Europeans to understand what life was like in that part of the world. Cook's claiming of new land for Britain allowed for the building of new British settlements.

Remembered Worldwide

Cook was mourned long after his death. The area in which Cook lived in England is now known as Captain Cook Country. The London home where Cook lived with his wife, Elizabeth, is now one of many museums that hold Cook **artifacts**, such as log books, items from his ships, and paintings by the ship's artists. A replica of the *Endeavour* was made to mark the **bicentennial** anniversary of Cook's voyage to Botany Bay. The ship has been sailed around the world, stopping in many places to educate people about the history of the ship.

Loss of Traditions

Cook is considered by many people as the explorer who opened up the Pacific, but many South Pacific Islanders see Cook as an agent of a foreign empire. After Cook, many European colonists arrived who pushed South Pacific Islanders off of their traditional lands or forced them to work on plantations. Europeans brought diseases, guns, war, and alcohol that destroyed the lives of many indigenous peoples. Missionaries encouraged them to worship the Christian god, and celebrate Christian holidays, such as Easter and Christmas.

Today New Zealand Maori teach their children their traditions, such as the haka, or war dance, in which men stick out their tongues to challenge each other.

-1788-

The British build the New South Wales colony in Australia, first at Botany Bay and then at Port Jackson.

-1801 to 1803-

Matthew Flinders, a British naval officer, maps the entire coastline of Australia, confirming it is a single mass of land.

-1824-

Australia gets its name.

(background) Captain Cook statue in Christchurch, New Zealand. The statue was created by William Trethewey, and has stood in the city square since 1932.

Glossary

aground Onto a shore, reef, or the bottom of a river

apprentice Someone who learns a set of skills from an expert

artifact An object, such as a tool, that can be used to study the past or a culture

astronomer A scientist who studies the stars, moon, sun, and planets

bicentennial A 200-year anniversary of an event

bribe To give something of value to someone for a special privilege

calculation A mathematical or scientific solution

Christian A follower of the teachings of Jesus Christ

colony A territory that is ruled by another country

convert To change, usually from following one religion to another

coral reef A hard rocky ocean ridge made by small animals over hundreds of years

course The direction or path that a ship takes

demote To bring down to a lower level of responsibility or authority

descent A shared family background

domesticated Animals that humans use, either for food, work, or as pets

dysentery A serious, painful infection of the intestines that is caused by drinking unclean water

eclipse The passing of a planet in front of the sun

inlet A bay between two landmasses

lieutenant A high position in the army or navy

log book A record book on a ship

malaria A disease spread by mosquitoes

marines Sailors that helped the captain maintain order at sea

missionary Someone who travels to various regions to preach a religion to the people who live there

navigate To direct the course, or direction, of a ship

New World North, Central, and South America

observatory A structure built for watching events in the sky, such as an eclipse

outlaw To make illegal

port A place where ships dock

provisions Supplies, such as food and water

sacrifice A religious ceremony in which something is killed and offered to a god

species A type of plant or animal

trade goods Valuable items that are exchanged for other items

viceroy A governor or ruler of a region or country

Index

1 2 3 4 5 6 7 8 9 0 Printed in the U.S.A. 4 3 2 1 0 9 8 7 6 5